Dog Breeds

Australian Shepherds

BY LIBBY WILSON

WWW.APEXEDITIONS.COM

Copyright © 2025 by Apex Editions, Mendota Heights, MN 55120. All rights reserved. No part of this book may be reproduced or utilized in any form or by any means without written permission from the publisher.

Apex is distributed by North Star Editions:
sales@northstareditions.com | 888-417-0195

Produced for Apex by Red Line Editorial.

Photographs ©: Shutterstock Images, cover, 1, 4–5, 8–9, 12–13, 14–15, 16–17, 18, 19, 20, 21, 22–23, 24, 25, 26, 29; iStockphoto, 6–7, 10–11

Library of Congress Control Number: 2023921622

ISBN
978-1-63738-903-4 (hardcover)
978-1-63738-943-0 (paperback)
979-8-89250-040-1 (ebook pdf)
979-8-89250-001-2 (hosted ebook)

Printed in the United States of America
Mankato, MN
082024

NOTE TO PARENTS AND EDUCATORS

Apex books are designed to build literacy skills in striving readers. Exciting, high-interest content attracts and holds readers' attention. The text is carefully leveled to allow students to achieve success quickly. Additional features, such as bolded glossary words for difficult terms, help build comprehension.

TABLE OF CONTENTS

CHAPTER 1
THE CHAMP 4

CHAPTER 2
RANCH DOGS 10

CHAPTER 3
AUSSIE TRAITS 16

CHAPTER 4
AUSSIE CARE 22

COMPREHENSION QUESTIONS • 28
GLOSSARY • 30
TO LEARN MORE • 31
ABOUT THE AUTHOR • 31
INDEX • 32

CHAPTER 1

THE CHAMP

An Australian shepherd jumps over a hurdle. Then he runs up and down a seesaw. The dog's name is Holster. He is at an **agility** event.

Agility events test a dog's speed and training.

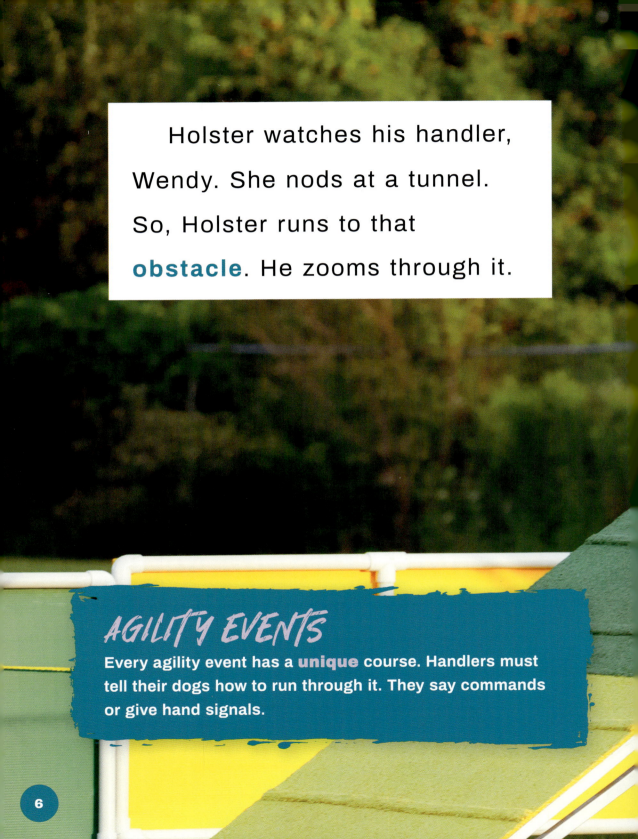

Holster watches his handler, Wendy. She nods at a tunnel. So, Holster runs to that **obstacle**. He zooms through it.

AGILITY EVENTS

Every agility event has a **unique** course. Handlers must tell their dogs how to run through it. They say commands or give hand signals.

Dogs watch how their handlers stand, move, and point. This tells the dogs where to go.

A set of weave poles comes next. Holster runs in and out between them. He crosses the finish line and jumps into Wendy's arms. His fast time wins the event.

FAST FACT

Dogs are scored on how fast they are. They must also do obstacles in the right order.

Dogs lose points in weave poles if they skip poles or go the wrong way.

CHAPTER 2

RANCH DOGS

Hundreds of years ago, Spanish farmers used dogs to move cattle. In the 1800s, some of these farmers moved to Australia. They brought their dogs along.

People have been using herding dogs for thousands of years.

By 1900, Spanish farmers had also come to California. They brought dogs, too. The dogs spread throughout western states. They became popular with cowboys and ranchers.

In western US states, most Australian shepherds herded sheep.

FAST FACT

Despite having Australian in their name, Australian shepherds are mainly found in the United States.

Aussies worked to guard and herd **livestock**. They also became popular pets. Today, the **breed** still helps ranchers around the world.

Herding dogs often help move animals through fields and into pens or barns.

HOW HERDING WORKS

Dogs control herds by running behind them. Dogs may nip the animals' heels and noses. Or they may bark. This makes the animals move or turn.

CHAPTER 3

Aussie Traits

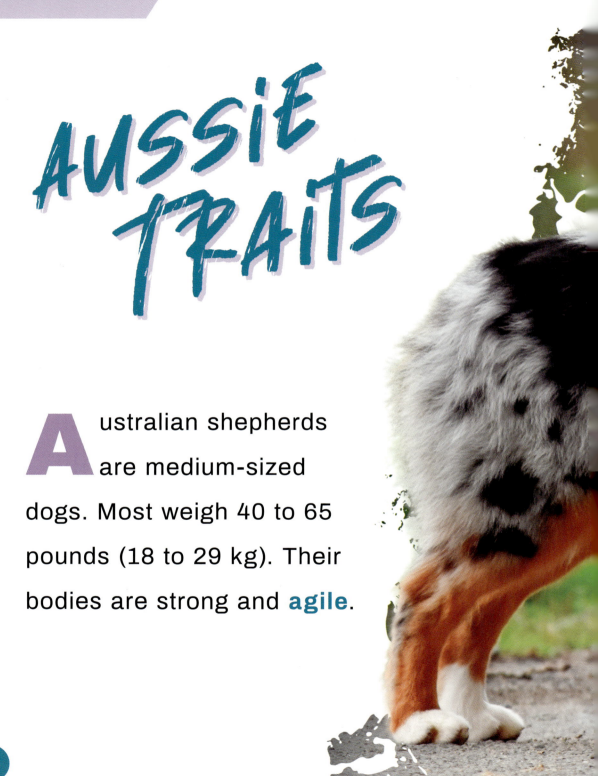

Australian shepherds are medium-sized dogs. Most weigh 40 to 65 pounds (18 to 29 kg). Their bodies are strong and **agile**.

Australian shepherds are 18 to 23 inches (46 to 58 cm) tall at the shoulder.

Tricolor coats are usually brown, black, and white.

Aussies' coats are thick and fluffy. Their fur often has spots or patches. The fur on a dog's neck and chest is extra long. This fur is called a mane.

FAST FACT

Merle coats have dark spots or patches on lighter backgrounds.

Blue merle coats have black patches on gray fur.

Aussies are more likely to have different colored eyes than other dog breeds.

SURPRISING EYES

An Aussie's eyes can be brown, yellow, green, or pale blue. In some dogs, each eye is a different color. This is most common in dogs with spotted faces.

Aussies were bred to do tough farmwork. They are smart and hardworking. As a result, Aussies learn tricks quickly. They are eager to please their owners.

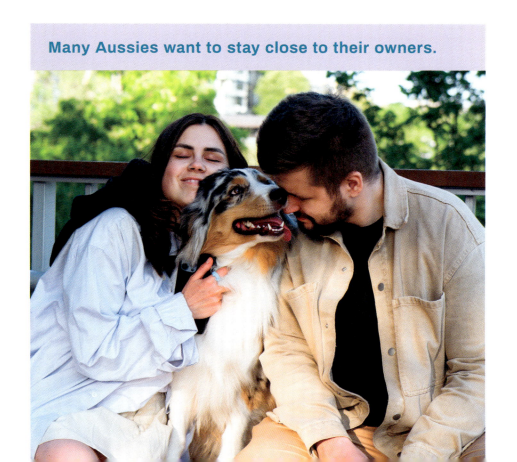

Many Aussies want to stay close to their owners.

CHAPTER 4

Aussie Care

An Aussie's fur can shed a lot. Owners should brush their dogs each week. Aussies also need baths every few months.

Aussies shed most in spring and fall. They need more brushing at these times.

Aussies need at least one hour of exercise a day.

Australian shepherds are energetic. They need to walk or run every day. Their minds need exercise, too. Owners should train them and give them toys.

Teaching tricks to an Aussie helps the dog's mind stay busy.

FAST FACT
Aussies may dig and chew if they grow bored.

Like many herding dogs, Aussies can be **protective**. They may also try to herd people. Owners can train them not to nip or bark. They should start when dogs are puppies.

EARLY TRAINING

Aussies were bred to guard, so they may be **wary** of strangers. Owners can have their puppies meet many people and pets. This helps the dogs stay calm around new things.

◀ Owners can start training their puppies right away.

COMPREHENSION QUESTIONS

Write your answers on a separate piece of paper.

1. Write a few sentences explaining the main ideas of Chapter 4.

2. Would you like to own an Australian shepherd? Why or why not?

3. What were Australian shepherds first bred for?
    - A. running in agility events
    - B. digging and chewing
    - C. herding animals

4. When did Australian shepherds come to the United States?
    - A. in the 1500s
    - B. before the 1800s
    - C. by the 1900s

5. What does **signals** mean in this book?

Handlers must tell their dogs how to run through it. They say commands or give hand signals.

- **A.** ways of making money
- **B.** ways of showing what to do
- **C.** ways to hold very still

6. What does **energetic** mean in this book?

Australian shepherds are energetic. They need to walk or run every day.

- **A.** active
- **B.** tired
- **C.** hungry

Answer key on page 32.

GLOSSARY

agile
Able to move quickly and easily.

agility
A sport where dogs run through an obstacle course.

breed
A specific type of dog that has its own looks and abilities.

livestock
Animals kept and cared for by humans.

obstacle
A thing that blocks the way.

protective
Likely to keep someone or something safe.

unique
Different from all others.

wary
Likely to distrust something, or likely to think that thing could be bad.

TO LEARN MORE

BOOKS

Kissock, Heather. *Australian Shepherds*. New York: AV2, 2022.

Pearson, Marie. *Dogs*. Mankato, MN: The Child's World, 2020.

Pearson, Marie. *Herding Dogs*. Mendota Heights, MN: Apex Editions, 2023.

ONLINE RESOURCES

Visit www.apexeditions.com to find links and resources related to this title.

ABOUT THE AUTHOR

Libby Wilson has loved books and reading her entire life. She enjoys researching and finding interesting facts to share with readers. Ms. Wilson enjoys watching agility events on her computer with her golden retriever Molly.

INDEX

A
agility, 4, 6
Australia, 10

C
California, 12

E
exercise, 24
eyes, 20

F
farmers, 10, 12
fur, 18, 22

H
herding, 14–15, 27

N
nipping, 15, 27

O
obstacle, 6, 8

S
Spanish, 10, 12

T
training, 24, 27

U
United States, 13

ANSWER KEY:
1. Answers will vary; 2. Answers will vary; 3. C; 4. C; 5. B; 6. A